UNHINGE CONSCIOUSNESS

Depression to the path of Enlightenment
before your 30s

UNHINGE CONSCIOUSNESS

Depression to the path of Enlightenment
before your 30s

Sam Nassiri

PAPER TOWNS
PUBLISHERS

PAPER TOWNS
P U B L I S H E R S

First published by
Papertowns Publishers
72, Vishwanath Dham Colony,
Niwaru Road, Jhotwara,
Jaipur, 302012

ISBN Print Book - 978-93-87131-42-2

Printed in India

Depression to the path of
Enlightenment before your 30s

*"This is a true story of my transformation of hell
on the outside whilst on the brink of depression
following separation and young family break up, to
gravitating toward the Kingdom of heaven within. For
the inner game of navigating your very nature of your
own body, mind, and spirit will aid your outer game
of monopoly and chess."*

Author, Reiki/ Energy Healer, Yogi

Contents

Introduction

The following account of my transformation, from once upon a time quite literally wanting to rip my hair out, to absurdly wanting to kiss the muddy surface of Mother Earth on a stormy day, is based upon a series of experiences occurred to me over the last few years in particular. My intent is not to teach you, but merely to supply you with information which could prove useful to you on your very own journey, based on my very own inner journey undertaken to date, which has resulted in an outer manifestation of self-discovery in ways I didn't ever believe or consider possible. I am currently writing in such a way, which is contrary to what I ever believed to be true. It is my honour to be able to connect with you and give you a profound insight based on my transformation. It is my wish and hope that I can be of loving service to you and to remind you that you are enough, worthy and limitless. I am sure my experiences presented in the following pages will go a long way in entertaining and inspiring you and people whom you consider as important in your life.

Mental Health, money, spirituality, and Brexit; these are all words we are hearing in the West today, permeated across news channels, radio stations, newspapers, default internet browsers etc. All serve their purpose, some may think. My perception has been altered by unfathomable experiences I encountered which led me to not only question all that I had ever been taught in my life but taking action into my own hands, call it initiative, to find out the truth, about the universe and the human psyche. With all my self-study, as well as a pile of strange and life-changing experiences, I have come to believe that penetration of the mind takes us into the sparse land of truth, the realm of magic. I for sure subscribe to the ideology or fantasy that heaven is right here on earth. It is for us to choose to notice it though.

The Concept of Existence

*T*his existence may seem unfamiliar territory or un-natural and at times impossible to some people, but really it is no different to the buds of the stem on the plant as it reaches to form into bouquets of roses. The flowers glow with aliveness, and then they die. Once again, they re-appear at their peak before dying. This process is unwavering, consecutive, and eternal. This is the battle of spirituality, the irony of learning to embrace both pain and pleasure (such as the oxymoron between thorns and petals) by way of equilibrium as it permeates through our experiences, some of us can live with the equilibrium, whilst others live in security by playing it safe to avoid pain and suffering if you will, whilst others simply suffer from allowing pain and suffering to get the better of them, failing to realise their limits when satisfying their egoic mind's deepest cravings, satisfying those little bosses who reside in one's mind, craving all kinds of physical or mental pleasures! Equilibrium of such pain and pleasure, on the other hand, defeats the double-edged sword of our existence, equilibrium comes from balance, moderation and abundance in our lives. We are able to live without becoming resistant. It is important to note that we still feel the intensity of the pain and pleasure, but we are grounded somewhere in the middle, watching on as a separate entity to any suffering, and we cease to give in to our desires which do not serve us. This requires a lot of work and self-inquiry, whilst others live in security or endless suffering, whether that is in the form of too much certainty or uncertainty in their lives. For someone who lives in a place of equilibrium, they do not have any such emotional home of fear, guilt and feeling constantly exhausted with life which most of us experience day to day. There a number of ways to live a life of balance and abundance, and there indeed are numerous methods of living free from pain and suffering, and not getting too attached with compulsive desires, as well documented in many books and preached by many great sages. A lot of which requires mastery over the faculties of the mind and understanding the flaws of our society, which creates an atmosphere where we are so immersed with our daily lives, that we hardly have any time to breathe properly, let alone take ourselves down for a massage!

What will
the Book
Do for You

*I*f you have opened this book to build yourself as an individual, or develop either physically, emotionally, mentally or spiritually or transform your sorrows and general every day hardships into a life of meaning or commencing or continuing your journey into enlightenment, then heart to heart, this book will change your life and also change the lives of those around you. I wouldn't want to bet against it at least. This is, however conditional, I must add. There are profound laws that are required to be understood, embodied and applied to enhance the harvest of such fruits, you will need to understand that this book does not promote or offer the same as a "get quick, get rich scheme", quite the contrary. It undoubtedly will allow you to take ownership of your worth and you will be able to cultivate strategies which will boost wealth and abundance in a more effortless and an at ease working methodology as opposed to the pushing type of motivation, which the wise deem to cause severe burn out and a complex lifestyle with minimal balance. This book is a story based on my own account of that which we commonly turn a blind eye to. To be more specific, it revolves around the higher calling we will normally receive once in our lifetime. In my case this was near enough depression, through to a transformation resulting subsequently in enlightenment, although I don't often like to refer to the word as "enlightenment", I prefer the expression of fulfilment or liberation, it is just that "enlightenment" is the main universal spiritual definition of the consequence of transformation and self-actualisation resulting from ignorance of the mind. There is often abstract conceptualisation in regards to the ego, and ignorance. These however can act as useful catalysts to our further growth toward multi-dimensional health, and thus in some respects ignorance is bliss, that's what helps us let go upon waking up. Before we proceed in discussing the true meaning of success and happiness, regardless of whether you are currently working at McDonalds cleaning toilets, or cleaning dustbins, or already running your own business, make no mistake that the person running their own business is not necessarily superior, more successful or happier than someone cleaning toilets at Mc Donald's. I am adamant, based on my very own experiences, and from having studied many successful influencers across the globe; that especially this thing called money is something we can easily let terrorise us at the best and worst of times. We are more than our payslip, we are more than our profession, we are more than our title, and we have enormous, boundless and relentless spiritual potential within us that can take us beyond the aforementioned. In fact, once you are aware of the elements you possess within you, you may come to realise that the most powerful weapon on earth is the soul on fire. Let me fill you in further.

I am 29 years old (likely 30 by the time it concludes) whilst writing this book and it has often perpetuated as a yoyo transformation for myself since hitting my early 20s. At times it has constantly felt like "2 steps forward, 3 steps backwards" for myself. Notably, when I was 26 years old, edging on 27, I had a young family to provide for whilst reaching remuneration in 6 digits (Pounds) in my second year of business in recruitment. I don't say this to impress you, but merely to express that money is not the "be all, end all" by any means. I most certainly do not wish to put you off the idea of seeking financial abundance, after all, I am sure you have bills to pay, potential debts that you owe, savings for your children or deposits for a mortgage etc. I am merely trying to express that my milestone of hitting 6 digits that particular year in fact equated to the most foolish, hellish (and some may call it Karmic) experience of my entire life to date. There was simply a lack of reverence in such period, which did backfire, to say the least. I subsequently lost my family, having come out of harmony with simple but ancient sacred laws of nature, you could call them universal truths. When one is posed a threat from non-balance and non-alignment both within themselves and outside of themselves; having worked too many hours or losing themselves to the expectations and pressures of careers, business, loved ones, relatives and friends (and yes they are important, but not to the extent of forgetting who we really are) then we could even lose all of the above. Such distortion clearly doesn't really positively outweigh the potential troubled outcomes resulting from stress, and thus rationally cannot be viewed as worthwhile or guaranteed. Fundamentally self-care, self-love and especially self-growth will be the biggest journey in your lifetime, so my message to you is not to get caught up on the money, on the mortgage, on a lucrative career, on luxury cars. Yes,

I happen to like these too, and I have also acquired some of these too. All it led me to was a genuine "slap in the face" from the universe. I recall separating from my fiancé and realising I had to start all over again, and it really did feel like a mountain to climb. I was worried about how I could influence my daughter, especially if I don't see eye to eye with my ex-fiancé's way of parenting, and it works both ways, by the way. This was by no means an easy situation and there were often times when I used to consider myself a failure. Separation or divorce is potent and brutal to one's well being in the immediate aftermath, and what makes it worse is the judgemental mindset of not only those concerned, i.e. close family memories, but also people not concerned who like to stick their noses in! Ultimately after hardship I decided to take charge by accepting that separation or divorce is bad enough, it's not an ideal situation, but salvaging your own spirit, and ensuring there is no divorce between yourself and your true self is essential. Separation was the starting point of a bright future, contrary to how our culture and society has a potent agenda to create a feeling of worthlessness and destruction to ones soul. Of course, it is far from ideal. Meanwhile, thankfully there is always a solution to our deepest fears and that is to face up with them. In a state of resourcefulness, in a manner of being solution and objective-driven, this is the privilege that life offers all of us, the power of choice to make a conscious decision to face the storm with the umbrella with courage. There is still a chance the umbrella may break in the storm, but by the same token, the storm could end at any moment since it is temporary. There are always risks, sometimes we have to take big calculated risks. Meanwhile, to conclude this introduction, I am going to kindly invite you to ask yourself

"Who would I be without my biggest worry?"

"Where would I be in my life without the worries I have accumulated to date?"

"How would I be to my loved ones and would I have more in the tank to give, pouring from a full as opposed to the empty cup, so to speak?"

Finding
the Meaning
of Life

*I*f you are starting to notice that you may be getting caught up on the material and maybe getting caught up under the spell of your mind (don't worry, this applies to all of us), then it may be time to consider finding deeper meaning and purpose in your life. This absolutely changed my whole life for the better, and at the time of writing this book, I earn half of what I earned 2 or 3 years ago which I describe as my pinnacle year of suffering. You are probably wondering how is this possible? Yes, I still have the same bills to pay, and child to provide for etc. The only distinction is simply because I have made it a priority to invoke freedom in my life. We need to cease buying into this illusion that having a successful career or making lots of money and working tirelessly brings us success and happiness. It doesn't bring us freedom though, something the human spirit longs for. A successful life is measured by others, not by our soul or heart.

Let's be honest, freedom in today's society has been lost, I say this collectively for many people, not for everyone. There are indeed those who have made this a priority which in turn allows for feeling like one has the extra time to make conscious decisions day by day. We have become too concerned and committed to simply fighting survival, or if we are more lucky than living a life of poverty, then we have got too caught up as a society on titles, labels, or chasing the money, or accruing assets and obsession with mortgages and also fashion, taking these to the extreme and leaving behind our connection to something of greater importance, which many of us are unaware of. Unfortunately, these accumulations and gains also require that we lose touch with our true nature. Our truest, highest version of ourselves need not attach to unnecessary personas. Many of the great sages, including religions and various ancient cultures, have made various and countless references to the Soul. You may have come across such references yourself, in fact, you may even be connected to the source of your being. The soul wishes to express itself for its true talents, which have been given to us as a blessing as part of our birth right. Some have referred to the soul as an inner compass per individual. Each one of us has unique talents and gifts to express and share with the world. However, most of us are living our lives in a JOB (just over broke) or entangled and consumed in the game of building assets and financial. There isn't anything wrong so long as there is a balance with other aspects of life which too can be integrated into one's lifestyle. However from personal experience and also having vigorously studied some of the most prominent, well-respected influencers in the world, it is well documented that it can be compared to gambling, at times you will feel powerful which is basically feeding your ego, and at other times you will lose money and not know when to stop. This is an example of an individual who is embedded in the money game, that they lose sight of the signs given to them by the universe to learn valuable lessons, or notice the new doors opened. I refer to these as the seeds of opportunity, and believe me they always tend to have a small window upon learning a valuable life lesson before they return once again. These signs are typically in the form of circumstances, but these often go missing and the cycle continues. I was in this place, but one day it took a major breakdown (some would call it a spiritual awakening, or Kundalini awakening) to finally make the change once and for all. I had 4 options looking back;

1) Continue downward spiral momentum and declining mental health (bottling up trauma, suppression, turns into depression, and depression leads to suicide. It's a horrifying cycle many of us face in today's world)

2) Continue as is, and hope for the best

3) Take massive action, hoping I am chasing the right direction and not going the opposite side of the sunset.

4) Remove my baggage upon recognising my egoic and logical traits, often referred to as the "shadow" or the "ego" the "intellect". Doing some "shadow work" to reclaim my spirit. Even the most enlightened spiritual teachers in the world still have to regularly cease to adopt these tendencies from re-occurring from time to time, so imagine how caught up and controlled by the mind the rest of humanity is!

We have virtually allowed our very own intelligence to turn against us. This is what has happened collectively and created many wars in politics and religion. People enhancing their intelligence but only in the category of the logical mind or intellect, which constantly makes the distinctions of "I am right, and you are wrong". We have effectively become set in our ways and may as well label our forehead with a tattoo of "it's my way or the highway". I believe that this example, combined with overconsumption and overindulging in our cravings and desires i.e. obsessive attachment to building assets and relying on material wealth to demonstrate our trophy of happiness has created what some often refer to as a cynical, divided, sick world. Your true nature is within you, buried somewhere waiting to be unleashed so it can emerge as your best self. It is in your best interests, in fact, you are under obligation from the universe or God, to damn right find out what this best self is like, and believe me, we all may think we know already, but we don't know half of it, because if you did, you would already be putting your neck on the line to be harmonious, loving and kind, not just to your friends and family, but also to your neighbours, co-workers and strangers, not to mention the 80% of the world who lives in true poverty in the world to make the world a better place. Changing the world may seem far-fetched or over-ambitious but nature requires all living creatures to transform and develop into fully-fledged creatures, human beings included. Besides, that extra love and compassion will surely be a step in the right direction to allowing for bonding like in romance, but in this instance, collectively with the emphasis very much on creating sheer, collective unity.

The quicker we come to terms with the flaws of our mind, and not just ours, but also the collective mind of society and media, also dubbed "the matrix" by many in our ascending modern-day rise, by those who are waking up to their sacred truth, then we will be able to free ourselves from the prison bars. In fact, going back to financial wealth, yes, we should indeed direct our focus and intention on accruing financial wealth so long as it is for the right motives which can create unity and equality as well as bringing more peace to those around us.

Do you still believe this is a tad far-fetched? Well okay, I did, until one day I opted to turn inwards and give meditation a shot after hearing several plaudits by major influencers whom I felt inspired by during my self-study. You may have heard of the likes of Tony Robbins and Joe Dispenza who have marvellous guided meditations and priming practices that will get you started. For those of you more advanced then look no further than those influencers or teachers of the ancient Eastern traditions such as the likes of Sadhguru and Deepak Chopra. These guys form part of the refreshing world elite who are bringing science, religion and spirituality together as it should be. If you are currently addicted to drugs, substances, alcohol and other disempowering habits and also find yourself locked in the mindset of eternal procrastination then I strongly recommend following Russell Brand on social media and look at his transformation. His journey is an inspiring one as clearly his recent books, podcasts and vlogs are that of a self-realised man expressing his true authenticity and I am sure he is the first to take responsibility for his down moments. Then again, he appears now to openly talk about his addictions merely being a case of losing connection, we often refer to someone as a "lost soul", I personally think there is definitely something in this.

Journaling

These days, even whilst writing this, I scrap down ideas on my notepad or journal my gratification, and on odd occasions, outrage to clear my thoughts and bring myself back to a level of feeling centred, and away from the restless senses and mind which can both become easily agitated without the necessary work required, and journaling is one of those rituals that works wonders to calm a fiery storm. It has been a great accelerator for my creativity and inviting my intuition to take over from my mind pursuits and all the psychological and emotional dramas. I do believe we all are co-creators, and more than our identification suggests. To overcome this, we can simply dis-identify or dis-label such title, so that we are nothing (or everything), or alternatively, it is just as effective to place any title next to our name we wish or choose. This may come across as too optimistic or positive thinking oriented, but believe me it works. You either have to identify yourself as absolutely nothing, which means you have subconsciously specified you have zero limitations or alternatively, you identify yourself as absolutely everything, which means you already have everything in some respects. Either or, are effective, as they both have a way of dis-identifying with your current identity. You could well be in a highly respected position culturally along with a PHD, for that I have the utmost respect for your achievements, but what is there to suggest there is necessarily a ceiling point to further achievements or milestones, not necessarily work or career related? What is to say there isn't more to come? What is to say that the person with the PHD treats others with the same kindness and loving respect or service for others, as say, the person who has no qualifications and less money? Everything in the universe is in essence a duality, so on one level if you think you are "nothing", you are actually "nothing" but also "everything", and vice versa. In the same way, the universe has been referred to as "nothing" and "everything". You are energy, and so is the whole universe. This is a confirmed scientific fact in Quantum Physics as some of you may already be aware.

To expand a bit more on my journal, or daily notes, I often write a list of all the labels I possess, and the list seems bigger, sometimes endless when I write it down in comparison to when I do not write. Writing is unquestionably a powerful tool to add to your arsenal since the sub-conscious mind takes kindly to things which are written down. The sub-conscious mind has a remarkable way of remembering things we write down that's for sure. This is how the manifestation of the non-physical to the physical occurs, for example, making a dream from our mind transcend to reality. I never believed I would run my own business for over 3 years whilst travelling the world and walking through the iconic, ethereal valleys of the Himalayas, but writing these ideas down and visualising them, or to be more specific, imagining myself experiencing these moments; have most certainly sparked a firework toward the stars. The stars, not to sound big headed, but more to realise that you already your very own star, whichever one you choose, that is when you do not limit yourself of course. Knowing your true worth is essential in both your rising prosperity and fulfilment of life. Once one comes to terms that they possess infinite potential, then very rarely do they stop rising. The infinite potential seems to have a way of showing up after our deepest levels of trauma as well. This is where it is the best time to plant seeds, as in every problem is a disguised opportunity. Some of the wealthiest investors on the planet have often pointed to investing during the periods of bust depression as their maximum opportunity to seize a strong profit. The fruit of the gains do not tend to show up immediately, so patience is very much a virtue whilst the nurturing and growth takes form.

In today's world, life is as challenging as ever, even with comforts such as technology, highest rates of mortality, access to external stimuli and fulfilling our mind's mini-bosses who all seem to crave something or another; whether that is a cigarette, food, sex, money, drugs etc. The list is endless, and these are simply neuro-associations we have considered to be pleasurable. These often fulfil our egoic desires as opposed to the longing of soul-destiny longing associated with our spirit. Such escape has been like a disease spreading in our communities, we have access to varying distractions and have become accustomed to this more than ever. Comforts and conveniences should really make life easier for us, but these are only short-term measures. Ever heard the saying, "getting out of your comfort zone" to stretch yourself further. We need to do things which challenge us to tap into our nature of resourcefulness. This is easier said than done, especially in particularly challenging times when we feel like the world is against us. However, this is also the time when we must dare to remind ourselves that life is happening for us, rather than against us. During the toughest of times, we still need to be pragmatic, finding gratitude when possible. There is always someone better off, but more importantly, there is always someone worse off. When you self-inquire on this, you can't deny that there is someone worse off, who could argue with that? If you find yourself stuck in the same old patterns, and struggling to make senses of life, then realise there is something beyond scarcity and more than our limits.

Emotions and Habits

*T*houghts can be taken as seriously as a blade of grass obstructing your whole day, only if you focus on it and allow it to, will it perpetuate and weed your consciousness and cause a paralysis effect to your beautiful and peaceful mind. On the other hand, I pay swift attention to emotions to ensure I am aware of bodily signals. The thoughts are external stimuli and conditioning, and as such, hence the need to watch them pass by without the need to attach any necessary action towards them, whilst emotions are a product of the body. Some of these emotions are so deep that it takes work to find the underlying root causes, this is where the practice of spiritual/ energy healing has positively impacted my awareness of filling some of the missing dots. Spiritual/ energy healing allows an individual to self-enquire very deep underground, and identify the roots, these roots refer to the entanglement of imprints, in other words, a memory of specific traumas which created a blockage in our sub-conscious mind, which by the way, is not our brain! It is actually another name for our body!

We will often feel emotions and identify and label them day to day, we are consciously aware of these which provides us with the privilege to follow through on these signals to take action of some sort i.e. loneliness could well be a sign to love yourself more, or to turn inwards and connect, it could even be a signal to call your relative or friend who you haven't seen in a while after a previous disagreement you had. Frankly, it could be several other things also.

Emotions which we are unconscious of, well these are memory patterns which take form as habitual behaviour, we need to look out for these and spot the signs if we can. I can completely resonate with this, as my habits over the years have included but not limited to nail-biting (that's from being a Tottenham Hotspur FC supporter!), sniffing, coughing amongst plenty of other things. My submissiveness has also dissipated. Thank goodness I feel freer and less compulsive these days. Often a relationship will bring out these habitual behaviours, after all, we are simply creatures of habit. Yes, in some ways like other animals. However, we are also the only earthly habituated creature that has an awareness which can make the decision to be more conscious and thus conciously change our very own reality and destiny. What an enormous, blessed opportunity this is when we can take a moment to let this in and feel it. We are therefore creatures of habit like animals; however, we also have, dare say it, "Godly" tendencies to create. We have a destiny here and a mission to fulfil. Even people who do not realise their mission, or do not believe in having a mission, still have a mission to get to the next stage of consciousness where their next mission will be officially unveiled. Or unofficially I should say! No-one has to know your mission but yourself. As conscious humans, some of us are aware of our purpose, and can easily think creatively, which works wonders for our imagination. By the way, fear is also imagination, as it is not assigned to the present. Fear normally is a past memory or experience which we are clinging on too so that we do not face the same pain again. We use the past to become anxious about the future which affects our decisions, and thus we forget our biggest power, the present. When we go back into the present, we tap into amazing qualities, our creative assets that provide us with aliveness and juice. It is in this time we have our largest power to create, as this juice fuels us with so much emotion. In the present, we become consciously aware of our habits and change this to less reactive based behaviour. In Hinduism, they define "karma" as a conscious action. Conscious action will bring out good karma, since a conscious person is not making "knee-jerk" decisions, nor are they operating from their ego or shadow self. They are simply being given instructions and guidance by the compass, or the guru within, spirit or "the soul".

Pathological Thinking

We have given far too much significance to our thoughts; this kind of pathological thinking is what sells our soul to the devil for most of us. Pathological thinking is a psychological drama. We need to master the inner work, and the way to do that is to firstly be aware of it, transcending unconscious reactive, knee-jerk patterns to more conscious actions. Being able to function consciously may not be easy, and as I said before it may be easier said than done, but it also means every moment of life is an exploration, this is frightening for some people. Rather than identifying ourselves with a label which we believe ourselves to be, or another person, it is better to not be identified with anything, literally "no identity at all". This welcomes other dimensions of perception and we are then able to view life in a new way; things will explode all of a sudden, in ways we didn't know possible. A good way to picture a comparison between living unconsciously or consciously is the difference demonstrated in creation, between animals and humans. Human potential is that of conscious action, whilst animals do not possess such conscious action, it is predominantly unconscious, survival flight or fight reactive actions. Humans have been blessed and granted the potential of living consciously, compared to their mammal siblings. Yet most of us live unconsciously, which means we are living like animals! Most of us live like animals, when really, we are biologically designed in such a way that we are able to reach Christ consciousness, through conscious action. Humans were therefore designed to touch this dimension of God, whereby a human being realises their connection with the one infinite creator. This is the journey of the self or the heroes' journey when one has to battle their mind in order to come to the realisation that they are conscious, possess free will, and are beyond their circumstances, the individual realises their superhuman competencies irrespective of past trauma or sobriety, and are then able to inspire others with their journeys as well.

When one is able to touch dimensions beyond the constraints of what we see in the matrix or in 3D reality, then it is likely they are reaching the higher chakras. Heaven is originally a code for the 7th Chakra, which will bring awareness, bliss, wisdom and enlightenment once activated, whilst, the lower chakras are more hellish in nature, which this is where the "Serpent of Fire" aka the "Kundalini Life Force" resides, and when aroused the energy is scorching hot and rises up the Chakras, towards the Heart Chakra, which where the road to the end of ignorance begins, the heart is ready to open. When the Fiery Serpent ascends the Chakras from hell to heaven (there are 7 in total), then this relates the individual to have a "second coming". The individual is quite literally born again! This type of consciousness is beyond the level of comprehension of most people understandably, given that we weren't really taught this in our 21st century schooling. This state of consciousness points to something that simply can't be conveyed by our level of mind. For myself, I have been in and out of these states for the last 18 months, and I believe it was as a result of being invoked by not fulfilling my soul purpose, being so out of alignment and dissatisfied with life in general, but by the same token there was still an eagerness for exploration. Some of us can reach heights by means of inspiration, and some of us can reach heights by means of desperation, whilst others can enhance their level of perception and have it fast tracked by both, I believe the latter applied to myself just to give you an idea.

How to Live Consciously

*G*oing back to the mechanics of how to live consciously and eliminate unconscious motives or actions, well when we are living and functioning unconsciously, we may not notice our behaviour until people around us, perhaps who live with us, or work with us or even by way of online communication will label our by-products of personality, and these people could well view these as traits or habits as a weakness, or an insecurity of some sort. It is important to note they may or may not be right or wrong. What is more important is that we use this as a catalyst to transform, as opposed to judging them in any way. Since really everyone we come into contact with is our biggest teacher or mirror reflection of self in some way or another. By judging someone for their faults, we are really at fault ourselves. The same goes the other way. The more mature and beneficial thing for your personal growth and happiness is to really take others' opinions with a pinch of salt. We should ensure that we avoid retaliating, and realise the other person is having a difficult time with their own healing, so they are trying the best they can based on their own challenging situations in life. Our desires shouldn't infringe on others free will, and if it is the other way around, then we should view them with loving compassion if we are able to do so. Otherwise we should move on from their toxicity, to ensure it protects our own wellbeing. Going back to the unconscious patterns of behaviour or what you or others may perceive as bad habits, could really be turned into a positive if you understand the mechanics of self-love.

Expectations

We are often blaming other people, or feel betrayed by other people because we have unrealistic expectations of them, especially the people we love. Of course, it works both ways also. We should respect they have their own free will, as do we. This conditional form of love is not real love. It creates pressure in one's identity, although that is our very own responsibility to take charge of. We know life can be difficult at the best of times, by battling with thoughts, feelings, emotions, judgements, impressions, sensations every day of our lives, so the least we can do is just be polite and kind to everyone around us. What we give out, will precisely return anyway. Unless you learn to face your own shadows, then you will continue to see such shadows in others, because the world outside you is really nothing more than a mirror reflection of your inner world. For example, try this judgement formula below. This is great for practicing your shadow work, and can give you significant insight into your inner world and help transcend your unconscious, judging behaviour which we all fall trap to sometimes;

If you are often referring to someone or people as idiotic, then try adding the words "so am I" afterwards. Likewise, if you are often referring to someone or people as beautiful, then try adding the words "so am I" afterwards.

I strongly believe that there is little need to take much notice of others' viewpoints as our very own perspective of ourselves is of greater significance. We could really do with giving ourselves regular health checks. I am not talking about physical health checks, and nor do I advise against physical health checks. This is more related to the source of a human being's issues, well before we pick up any physical ailments. This notion is mainly related to purely mental, emotional and spiritual by way of self-inquiry. The science of Yoga refers to the non-physical source of health also. When we are balanced within, which involves loving ourselves, and the opinion we place on ourselves, not living in guilt or fear, and with our balanced masculine and feminine energies within, then we are a perfect fit for re-union with God. The word "God" can easily be misinterpreted but what they mean is the universe or nature or love or life.

When we are in harmony with nature, things seem to flow much more effortlessly, I am sure you can relate in one way or another? You see, self-love is our nature. What we call "God" is "Love". What we call nature is "Love". Everything points to love at the end of the day. So, if we can't love ourselves, then what chance have we got of loving other people. It is not as easy as loving other people if we can't love ourselves firstly, as we lose vital life force energy. Yoga is a way of aligning our energies so that we can be in balance. Being in balance virtually means we are accessing self-love and we realise the only boundaries we have set are limitations to bond with others as we hadn't self-loved before the practice of Yoga. Yoga is not the only way, but most definitely one route. Nature is another, as is meditation or prayer. You come to realise you are more than just your body. An old person with a broken-down body still could have a wild heart to live exuberantly compared with a strong bodybuilder who could be at discomfort with their emotional, mental and spiritual wellbeing having paid more attention to their body which only equates to one part of the person, for it is the consciousness and mind which drives the machine. Connection with the source within creates profound knowledge, which is likely to create an execution of trillions of cells working positively, going a long way to easing your body-mind.

The deeper we dive inwards, the more exposure to these roots of these behavioural patterns that create our subconscious emotions. We have by large, mastered the transformation of the unconscious to conscious action, one in which can step beyond pain and suffering at least, a bit more than before. This sounds like a bit of hard work, but like anything, practise makes progress (not perfect). Eventually mastery!

The individuals mastering this concept has already began their journey to freedom, in fact, by reading this book, and reaching this point, you have already began constructing the foundations!

Bringing forth and transcending your unconscious behavioural patterns into conscious action by way of heightened awareness is life-changing for yourselves and also potentially in others, in the sense that not only will you notice others respond with your noticeable actions, but more importantly, you will feel the spark of momentum and progress, the willpower button will be well and truly switched on like fuel gas. This has enormous benefits for your pre-frontal cortex which is the part of your brain which produces neurotransmitters and can extend its capacity and essentially magnetising a tiny pea of willpower to the return of a cricket ball, the more you tap into willpower, the more power you get back!

Meditation

$\mathcal{I}$ mentioned self-inquiry and turning inwards, these are so closely linked to the ancient wisdom traditions of the East, whatever happened to meditation and breath work over the years and why it hasn't been an option provided at school, let alone a mandatory practice for children as per the ancient teachings of schools of virtually most religions and cultures, I personally will never fully be able to comprehend I don't think. Meditation is your call to freedom. Freedom yearns you, and you obviously yearn freedom, I am sure? The same could be said with respect to your soul-bonding connection. There is no better avenue than to break away from the chaos and publicity into silence, solitude and nature. If you are worried about being in isolation or silence, believe me, it can get dangerously addictive. Like cancer, silence and solitude tend to grow quickly. This adjustment of ritual in my life, of spending more time alone away from the midst of usual distractions, several years prior to writing this is by far my biggest growth spurt!

I came to realise that meditation is not only about training your mind or calming your mind. It involves every cell in your body. It consists of the world around you as much as it does within you even though you have broken away from the world around you. It involves the invitation of your mind working as a servant to your soul, the spirit. It involves transcending unconscious to more conscious patterns of behaviour as previously mentioned. This transformational process of transcending unconscious patterns of behaviour to conscious based is quite literally giving your brain a whole new software upgrade and download of information, as well as coherence between your heart and mind. You also become introduced to the chakras. Meditation is the treasure map that can miraculously give a hug to the person that is meditating, feeling a deep intimacy with the source (what some people believe to be God). There is most certainly still some work to do and challenges you will hit, except you will have more clarity in the face of uncertainty. Perhaps clarification that life is one big giant bundle of uncertainty, so dance with it and follow your heart. It has been said that meditation leads to the language of God, divine whispers from the source of our creation. For this world to exist, there would have been a creator (even if that was a big bang, something would have created the big bang), there is a creation also (which is the universe and all the physical matter you see around you, whether that is natural terrain or skyscrapers), and there is life such as animals and humans (which was made by the creator, in the same way, a mother biologically conceives and creates a new born baby, they are both so connected). Meditation brings all these facets together as one, for there is really no difference between the creator, creation and the children of the creator, as they all are an intrinsic part of creation itself. Creation required all these facets, as creation is simply expressing itself in a process. We are sub-particles of the one infinite Creator and thus we are all co-creators and can create what we imagine, the universe will take care of the rest of the details when we set our intentions. Our connection to the universe comes from being connected to the source. Meditators and Yogis, including myself, believe the universe reveals its secrets to those who dare follow their hearts.

Clarity also comes in the form of knowing you're on the right path. I am not writing this to advise you what to do, or which direction to head toward, nor should you listen to anyone. However, the case study demonstrating the significance of a mass meditation and its subsequent effects on humanity is astonishing, to say the least, and although the recorded episode of 7,000 people performing a mass meditation and bringing crime, terrorism and other forms of inhumane activities is somewhat surprising. On the other hand, it is not really that surprising when one observes the way our modern western societies are run today, to ensure the masses of population are controlled, again I refer to this as working in a JOB (Just over broke) as a function of the matrix (adhering to the cultural rules of society like every Tom, Dick and Harry). We eventually break out of this trap, you could call it a scam, as well when we begin to question why we are not advancing at the same rate as others, this then attracts you to study those in which you perceive as successful, such people then offering you a sample of their thinking as you begin to model their rituals and follow their morals. Eventually, the growth of consciousness begins to expand, and the individual begins noticing they are more than just a number. As a kid, it was simply your world to explore, why should it not be any different today or tomorrow? If you as the reader oblige me to give you any advice before reaching the end of this book, then it will be to endeavour to meditate when you can, or more often than you currently do. I would recommend ideally at least 15 minutes in the morning, and 15 minutes before turning your lights out before sleep. Whilst meditating, remain patient, and if you get stuck or have any queries then feel welcome to locate me via social media where I perform live and recorded meditations. I will do my best to respond back promptly although I do not like giving promises! There are also a number of others who you could follow as well. By incorporating meditation as a daily practice, you are going to open the beautiful garden of your mind where it is full of seeds, as opposed to a messy weed garden. Your perception will be both sharpened and broadened. If it is the transformation you are seeking, then meditation will enable you to take charge of this as well as learning about your life force and energies. The doorway to your soul will open and the instructions of your future will become apparent. This can be a shock to the system at first, not to put you off the idea, it is more a case of time to introspect just how much you would like things to change. Meditation will bring you the opportunities and clarifications you need to burn your habits and desires which distract you from your goals. Some goals will be re-set and the bar raised. The same rituals and habits of behaviour produce the same results. It's a hard fact to swallow. If your life to date, has been to predominantly to keep away from danger and for striving for security, then prison indeed meets such requirement. Often times we are stuck, or we feel stuck and that is what makes us stuck, it is an illusion, we are actually free, always have been and we always will be, however by the very nature of our mind, and all of its intelligence, we have collectively, and often also individually turned it against ourselves, and we have lost the user manual. There is a simple key with the instructions and that comes in the form of meditation to seed human consciousness, both individually and collectively. Otherwise, we are stuck with the limitations of a stagnant rigid vehicle as our mind. We all deserve an upgrade! Logic, will always aid our imminent survival, but the notion that we have enormous superpower capabilities to envision a dream and manifest that energy and intelligence into the matter are definitely not from our logic, don't you think? Every man-made construction of an object, buildings, towns and cities were first emanated from the arousal of dreams, which were then presented as architecture on a piece of paper, before the final important step, the long waiting, nurturing the planted seed, going through the darkness of night. I believe we all know somewhere deep down that there is always light at the end of the tunnel. Forget money, and I am sure God, or the Universe will bless you with it when God or the Universe feels it is necessary. When you make money, then God will only want you to give it away to promote equality away from the constraints and discrimination we already have.

Financial abundance always takes care of itself when we are placing our focus on enhancing the level of our consciousness and perception, living out our purposeful passion. Whoever told you that you have to be a millionaire in order to live a successful, happy and fulfilled life sent you to the wrong destination! I get for some of us, including myself, this could well have been a close relative, such as parent, guardian or sibling. There is no destination other than embodying love. You are a vessel of love when you are expressing your true spirit. People will bow back down to you with love when they can notice your joy and integrity as a sumptuous combination.

Love is currency, yes, money is referred to as a currency, but ultimately it is what you do with it when you have it. So typically, when we don't have it, we need to have gratitude for the things we often forget and take for granted, therein lies the true treasure. It is once again going back to that same old notion that we bring our unconscious insecurities out to the open as a conscious behaviour, so that in which we are back in control of the powerful mind. Perhaps deceiving is a more appropriate word as we don't want to give the mind too much respect, do we? We can use our endeavour to limit our subconscious mind so that we are only on autopilot whilst we are driving! Oh no, I wouldn't recommend that either!

The purpose is simply to heal your wounds, not just physical, but to heal your deepest, darkest fears and insecurities. Those deep-rooted fears I once had and know many others have of simply not feeling worthy enough, the need to people please, live to others expectations; particularly their deadlines. Money is often something we view to demonstrate our success, nothing wrong with that but if we have over-invested our attachment, then we are no longer living in the present, we are merely fearing our imaginary future based on feeding our fears which have simply emanated from our wounds which are nothing more than past memory associated. Focus on the now and watch what happens! Grace likes to take care of the rest. The rest is purely ego constructs, and we will free ourselves from breaking away from this massacre! It has been well documented by many mystics that when their awareness is set in the present, they are able to notice signs from the universe and the chances of synchronicities rapidly increase. The universe is always sending us signs, but it is virtually impossible to notice the robin that appeared next to your patio door if you are too busy worrying about what happens to your laundry if it rains! There are no coincidences since every event we experience and people who come into our lives for a short time, or long-duration have been intentionally put in our path to help raise our level of awareness and enhance the consciousness of the collective. Yes, you heard that right, what I am saying is that there are no such thing as accidents, in our universe!

Think about the all-time greats, the Nelson Mandela's, Mother Teresa's, the Mahatma Gandhi's for a moment; these were people who lived a life filled with grievence, sense of loss, betrayal, pain and suffering like all of us will face from time to time, however they were able to transcend all of this to love, give, serve and share as the history books reveal to us. Their very own conciousness would have blossomed like the transformation of a seed through its very own darkness, stuck in the soil with barely any direct sunlight. They were also known to have resurrected and transformed on the back of their circumstances. Many people in their shoes, in fact, the majority of humanity would have become a victim of circumstance had they been in the midst of their situation. They were not superhuman, and if they were, so are you too. The only difference is that they cultivated the pain and suffering as a catalyst of pure drive, grit and determination. They did not rely on or place their eggs in one basket, and by that, I am explicitly referring to the concept of the pursuit of financial abundance alone. Instead, they realised there is no greater gift to wake up each morning to see another day. Another day, to make an impact. We surely serve a purpose; otherwise, there is no justification as to why we are here, that doesn't make sense at all.

No wonder why we feel overworked and drained of motivation, we have collectively lost meaning in our lives, that fundamental which trumps solely financial success hands down. The great Tony Robbins often refers to the notion that there is the "Science of Achievement" and also the "Art of Fulfilment" which are the two main jigsaw pieces to feel diverse, balanced and whole, such wholeness would make up a perfect definition of success. Of these two expressions, it is the "Art of Fulfilment" that is more integral than the other. Many people, including myself have had a taste of the "Science of Achievement", soon realised that is all they have come to know and have forgotten the important stuff such as internal wellbeing, which requires an understanding of our inner engineering. Tony Robbins, on several occasions, has mentioned the name Robin Williams (I adored and idolised him as a child growing up) but ultimately in spite of having what we would often culturally perceive as everything, a loving family, beautiful children, and having the natural ability to make people laugh as a world-class actor/ comedian. However, he was unable to overcome depression which usually requires years of suppression of emotions, or bottling it up as some people would call it. He was considered successful by many, but mastery of thoughts and emotions haunts most of humanity today, and very often it is the very successful people who have lots of money and fame.

We have to make time to love ourselves, to heal our wounds, as I said previously in this book – investing in oneself is the biggest investment anyone would make. It is the soul's natural desire to long to be the best it can be, that's for certain, otherwise, there would be no such definition of destiny. However, if we are not conducting our mission in accordance with the soul's instruction, then this neglects our connection to the source. This then begins to take its toll on both, the mind and the body, because in essence, they are the same thing. The human nervous system and physical body would benefit by being cultivated in the same way as a temple is treated by worshippers. It is a teaching mechanism and an exquisite pharmacy, able to heal you if you let it do its job the right way. Wear and tear and ageing are inevitable, but we can look after it well, in such a way Yogi's are able to boast. This sort of thing needs to be better publicised in communities. I genuinely believe (and this is now my very own mission and life's work to demonstrate) that this is why mental health is a hot topic. We have reached a peak for suicidal deaths in the Western World in the last decade, in particular, this is a catastrophe considering we have created many conveniences and comforts in this modern, digital age. Unfortunately, by the very nature of such conveniences and comforts, they have enabled us to rely on such things more than our wellbeing as a priority. We live in a technological box world, from mobile phones, I-pads, TV's, car, to the cinema theatre, everything is a box these days. In fact, it's not just technology, it is also the food we eat, the carton we drink out of and the packet of painkillers we treat ourselves with. Going back to the suicide statistics over the last decade, this is alarming and catastrophic, clearly showing that we haven't gone forward in human evolution despite such creation of comforts which are supposed to be of convenience and of support. Something's gone wrong, hasn't it, surely?

This is an alarming call to action, to not only speak out, but to study about the self, and by that, I mean your mind, also consciousness, spirituality and the universe. This is most definitely a rabbit hole, but it is also a doorway into bringing the unknown into our awareness. Typically, as humans, we are fearful of the unknown. In my experience, the unknown and uncertainty pushes one on the edges of what that individual can truly tolerate by stepping through it, anyone you may know who is courageous by nature, is not immune to being afraid, they are no different to most people. In fact, the only difference is that they measure up the questioning concept of "what have I got to lose". This is the beauty of the eternal spirit; it wants you to find stability in uncertainty itself. Uncertainty is the subtle and precise doorway to abundance and security!

Every one of us has been blessed to be a human being when we take into account their jaw dropping odds of a 1 in 400 trillionth chance of being here as a human being! Now that is what you call a true reminder (or kick up the backside, however way you wish to put it) of putting your life into perspective!

We all somewhere within us know, that there is a space of greatness, pure wisdom, strength, humility, compassion, and magic. I believe all these superpower qualities are sub-particles together forming divine love, the power of love given to us by God/ the Universe. Energy of pure intelligence to enable us to grow and flourish in life. This can take time for most of us. In the same way, a lotus flower is not fully grown until each petal has grown one by one, eventually, though, it all pans out in divine timing! The divine love, which is always available to us when we open our hearts and mind, and the necessary space by renouncing all toxicities, resides as a candle waiting to be lit. The trouble is that we can't light the candle if we don't know how to, or we don't know where the candle is!

Your true self and primordial genius are ready to be tapped into and expressed by way of ongoing meditation and/or time spent in silence, ideally solitude. You will be able to see everything and everyone around you through a whole new lens. This transformed my life. It transformed many sages, prophets, entrepreneurs, teachers, healers, and enlightened masters to the same conclusion, and by the conclusion I mean the beginning of something new, call it death, death of the self, subsequently followed by re-birth. You can do the same also. I believe every single one of us could be a healer and lightworker on behalf of this wonderful world where we are all interconnected. You are no different from your greatest idol, so why not model their behaviour, and before you know it you will adopt their traits perhaps? Let's not forget we all bleed the same blood, breathe the same oxygen and drink the same water.

Meditation is a beautiful way of meeting your inner guru of what some books and scriptures refer to as the "Higher Self". We all have a future and best version of ourselves, beneath years of memory and conditioning embedded in our DNA. The idea behind Yoga and meditation is that it is renowned to allow an individual to experience, witness and observe the present, and thus leaving the past behind. Most of us are locked in the past without even realising how detrimental this is to our soul, that sacred part of us embedded beneath all such conditioning and memory. I cannot count enough times the benefits now scientifically proven to be associated with meditation, to be able to break away from the chaos and stress of everyday life and alter one's brainwave states such as theta and delta, which heighten the mind's focus, creativity and connection to receiving universal downloads from higher intelligence. This is as good as a system upgrade to your whole being! Why turn to drugs or alcohol or other forms of escape when you can simply escape from the chaos, nonsense or mundane, however without the self-sabotage feature of one's journey and more so a seeded as opposed weed approach en route to growth, expanded awareness, equanimity, tranquillity and concentration. The only thing I would say is that meditation has a certain feel of addiction. Much like other forms of escape once you acquire the release of certain neurotransmitters. This will explain why an artist cannot stop producing works of art, and a writer producing articles and books, and a musician selling new records. As I write this and mentioned recently in one of my recent social media posts, that for all the times I have set goals and at times failed and succeeded both respectively, I have felt the larger growth from what I considered as failures at the time, and on that note, I do not put too much emphasis onto setting specific goals as I have one goal, and one goal only, and that is to follow my heart's desire, which is merely guidance reaching out as emotion. This is the intelligence and beauty of the soul fulfilling the obligations and responsibilities as the soul to express its unlimited talents, and infinite potential. Both of us (as in yourself and I) have been blessed with this boundless power. The moment we define a list of goals, as much as it is better than being lethargic, and not taking any action at all, or having any vision at all, it will produce mediocracy. For example, by goalsetting you may temporarily feel good when the goals are hit, but how would you ever know what could have been, had the one goal alone, been to be your best version? It is one simple goal to set, isn't it? Nothing complicated, no thinking on how to get there, the soul responds well to this goal as if a button has been pressed and held for a few seconds until the soul is ready to say, "thank goodness, finally you are ready, now let me give you some extra help". Ignorance is immediately dispelled, as the individual is well and truly ready to do whatever it takes to begin their spiritual journey on the same road as their sacred destiny. All of a sudden, by setting this undeniable priceless goal, there is a potency to your game. You want to be the very best version of yourself, so you have already ceased the competition around you by only focusing on yourself, not getting involved in the handbags with other folks. You have the fuel and juice, that pull-motivation you could also refer to it as pure passion from the powerful heart. This has enormous effects on the world around you. You are already bending reality by cultivating a higher form of intelligence, than the 95% who haven't reached your level of awareness as yet. Don't get me wrong, some will infectiously be attracted to your shining bright light of living, wise and joyful qualities and naturally, inherit these and make them their own, as energy and love has a boomerang effect insofar as what you put give out, always comes back accurately. If I were to go back and track everything I gave out, most of the stuff I gave out, has most certainly come back to me, alright that's for sure! I am quite sure there is more to come as well! This scenario is referred to as the Law of Karma. The people you come into contact with will be inspired and empowered and they will spread such love and light to others, think how much peace can spread across our communities just by making a few tweaks and alterations to our lifestyles, beliefs and values. Don't worry so much about the action as that comes itself and tends to propel naturally, upon true inner self-love, that harmony and peace within yourself, that connection to source, as I keep saying, our very own birth right. Every single one of us is already enough, contrary to your own false limiting assumptions, beliefs and stories you may have made up for yourself, can you relate at all? Let's not go into other people's judgements, remarks or opinions, the latter put me through hell and back for a good few years during my mid 20's (ironically and coincidentally the most prone age for male suicide). That need to compare with others, as much as social media has an array of pros and benefits, there are of course, some

59

aspects which require some caution and attention on. It is easy to identify someone or many people who are richer, skinnier, muscular, younger or older than you and I, but how can we possibly judge as to whether they have darkness, major insecurities and difficult situations and circumstances in the background, how are we supposed to know that individual who is ever so skinny and fashionable whom looks the part, didn't have an underlying childhood, teenage or early adulthood condition such as anorexia, or an eating disorder of some kind? I am not saying we have to agree to anything as such, we are always quick to judge or blame one another, as we have been caught in this natural cycle of humanity today. As mentioned before, we have turned our very own intelligence against ourselves by way of not using the user's manual to our mind, which has resulted in most of us having a dormant functioning brain, believe me, it is being neglected and up for misuse every time we race to get to our mobile as soon as we wake up each morning. I am by no means implying that our brain has gone dead, as in actual fact that would probably be a whole lot better and restrict overall restlessness and compulsiveness, something which our mind loves to cling to at the best of times! I would instead imply, that it is more a case that putty has been left off its lead and it has an array of opportunities in front of itself, only to make a catalogue of messy errors, picking at all sorts of things unconsciously! This is how our thought process and the never-ending cycle of judgements have evolved into today. Another thing we could consider if we were more conscious and stepping behind our thoughts and judgements, on others I mean, is that person you deem as supposedly blessed, or "lucky", naturally talented and successful has very likely been given the same number of life trials and tests as you or I have,. After all, they are human too, and human beings are surrounded by problems. As the saying goes by Les Brown "You are either in a problem, or you have just come out of a problem, or you have about 12 heading towards you!"

As a soul you have a permanent existence, so thus your existence is not theoretically subject to birth and death as you know it, the body will shut down and die, but your soul will live on, such as the nature of this omnipresent energy. As a soul you are free to believe in whatever you wish as comfort, however, if you aren't already aware, I would like to point you in the direction of the exploration of Modern day science, Quantum Physics which is not necessarily mainstream as we know it, that said it is becoming well publicised as top Scientists are now placing a huge emphasis on investigating the fathom concept of consciousness. One thing we can be sure of to date is that there have indeed been various studies to prove that when an atom is broken down, it is absolutely nothing in physical form, other than pure energy. Such energy contains significant amounts of cosmic intelligence. You, my friend, are pure energy and I will leave this topic as that for you to work out the rest if you are not entirely sure of the magnitude of this exciting piece of factual notion. I cannot reveal much more simply as it is not my job to disclose something sacred to your very own journey, my experiences are my experiences, and your experiences are your experiences, we can only help one another based on our experiences and also, with the assistance of studies to back up each of our perspectives. Fundamentally, both of our jobs is to endeavour to connect the dots, which can at times appear as never ending, since we live in an infinite world after all. What you have knowledge of based on this topic, unfortunately, won't be discovered by most of the population of the world until retirement. Personally, if I had one regret in my lifetime, it would be that I lived my life psychologically and spiritually blindfolded and ignorant, going to my graveyard having not discovered my talents and shared it with those around me. I think that would be a genuine, tragic pity on my part if I didn't test my limits to see how far I can go, and I don't mean by how many followers or friends one has on social media. I have maintained such a pool of loving souls as localised and compact, as that works for me and nor do I pay much attention to audience, as I choose to let God/ The Universe take care of the rest. Generally, when I blog or vlog, and share wisdom based or awareness content virally, I do it out of passion and am happy in the comfort of knowing it has helped even just one soul. That soul may have a larger audience. That soul has its own unique destiny, and yes that soul may well, or may not well, be yourself. There really isn't any competition, since we are all, at the deepest level beneath our physical bodies, all one source. Isn't it marvellous to know that we have boundless and infinite potential?

For myself, I have a fear of public speaking, and it doesn't feel right, so it clearly doesn't align with my longing desires, which are that of the soul, whereas writing is more my thing. For you, my dear reader, you may be an artist, or musician, or whatever, only your soul truly knows. Whatever our unique talent is, it will help the world unfold like the lotus flower petals, but there are also some similarities we each share, and that is to heal by way of inspiration and sharing of our sacred, unique gifts once we have discovered and developed this passion. Once we come to terms with what it is exactly, then I happen to feel it's an obligation otherwise a divine blessing of pure grace being given to us by God/ The Universe has gone to waste, and someone or a group of people will require your help somewhere down the line. This talk of grace or blessing is that of the higher will or call it God's will if you prefer. However, you perceive it, it really is something beyond our mind's comprehension and it is very unique, that's for sure. In order to really find out what our gifts, talents and passions are, it is good practice to get ourselves out of the way and let the intuition guide us. This requires self-reflection, self-inquiry, Yoga, Meditation or time spent in nature to really open this channel up. We are then able to distil the love and wisdom within ourselves, exercising our imagination. Once we have been instructed by the whispers or unique synchronistic communication by our intuition, as the universe is always speaking to us by way of communication, then we are well equipped to express what we truly feel, without shame or fear, this is being a leader of the heart. Western culture today and the society most of us live in doesn't really encourage us to find own path, and we instead unfortunately blindly believe what we are told from a young age, whether that is by way of guardianship or schooling. It continues throughout adulthood as well, especially in the workplace and the "Lion's Den" in the playground when dropping the kids to school! Such fear of being alienated or loneliness dates back to the Animal Kingdom or in ancient times when humans lived in villages and tribes. For example, if one person left, then that person would be stuck in the desert, which has undoubtedly continued to propel in today's society as well.

With the awareness that we at times inherit such fear, due to our social conditioning and hypnosis, the environment and particular people around us who do not necessarily serve our highest purpose, we are able to step into our truth, that burning desire to speak out for what we believe in. Before we proceed to this scale, it is always better to ensure that we speak with truth and honesty in a way that is loving and constructive. There is likely to be some opposition at times, as it is often those who are not free that view true freedom and authenticity as being negative or evil. As always, with such opposition, it is always beneficial to shine the torch of love, respect and compassion.

Ultimately at some point, we will come to terms with our true, deep feelings as we heal, especially when we have meditated or practised Yoga, spent time in nature etc. There comes the notion of free will. Without having a crystal-clear vision, it is sometimes difficult to avoid falling into confusion, doubt, frustration and self-pity. These then contribute to a question to oneself of identity, which isn't necessarily a negative thing, for this challenge and darkness begins the process of shedding snake skin. It is at this point, we begin to turn even further inwards. I have been through this cycle several times, and it is indeed painful, yet rewarding, but patience must be cultivated, as seeds often blossom to a thousand forests at the right season, so wait patiently for the right season and it will be completely worthwhile! Things will start to make sense, and it is normal to want to dive even deeper or dig deeper down the rabbit hole to discover more hidden truths, both with oneself, as well as the secrets of the universe. There is various inexplicit material, some of which can be misleading with varying perspectives causing some confusion when we come to study, so it is always best to consciously select which extracts of information one wishes to place in the beautiful garden of their mind. It is great to be optimistic and open-minded, but not to the extent of leaving oneself exposed. There are indeed conflicts of information so step forward with awareness and caution, balanced with your open mind and that should stand you in good stead. A paradox example of misleading perspectives which somewhat baffled me previously was that some Spiritual Teachers/ Influencers claimed the answers are all within, whilst others claimed the significance of finding a reputable, tailored Spiritual Teacher/ Healer of Guru to help with the journey of an individual facing hardship, or an individual wishing to develop spiritually and psychologically. Based on my very own perspective, I believe it is a case of simply dancing with both notions, balance and moderation is always a good place to reside. There is no doubt that the answers and true wisdom are embodied within. However, because we have been raised in 21st century schooling and we are generally living at distance from our true nature, when we reach the point of self-realisation or awakening, it can arise very intensely, and too much for one without the necessary guidance. So certainly, in the early days, it is pivotal. Before we learn to drive, we typically have driving tests to get used to driving. This is a great metaphor for how we learn to channel our Chakra (energy centres). I would strongly recommend joining a Yoga class for this is a great tool and insight to balance and ground the energies which one occupies. I have personally implemented learning both via my intuition, and externally via respectable spiritual teachers, healers and gurus. I am not one to make too many conclusions in a world whereby we are always later proved wrong in our conclusions, but based on my own experience I feel that it is safer, even if it is costly financially in the beginning, to find one of the aforementioned to mentor and handhold until you find your feet. They can really inspire you to meet your higher self, which is much like your future self, your inner guru, which has access to cosmic intelligence, the universe. I feel an experienced, wise mentor is integral, much like a parent sculpting their new born child, except in this case, aiding an individual of whom are either striving for to progress their level of perception, knowledge, experience and evolution to the next level via either desperation or inspiration. For me it was a blend of both as it were, and both indeed require extravagant masses of support as I did too, this could be on the back of trauma or depression or disconnection from source/ God, or it could be a result of seeing others around the individual going through the journey of enlightenment, which is sure to beg the question of the individual, and there is no option but the start of an awakening. In my case, a very intense awakening often referred to as "The Dark Night of the Soul". I felt I was left with very little choice but to explore the avenue of finding a Spiritual Healer who could answer my 101 questions. The only other choice was to continually sabotage and crumble and who knows, may even have potentially ended up in a hospital if I continued to descend emotionally and psychologically in a downward spiral. I believe our hospitals and Medical/ Mental Intuitions in the Western countries, sometimes ignorantly, inaccurately and knee-jerkingly label people who have encountered a deeply spiritual experience as a mental condition. This can be a complete un-just misdiagnosis, and requires further investigation into the topic. There is no better time than now, for science, spirituality and religion to merge. There is a lack of exploration in spiritual awakenings when it comes to our systems and institutions in the Western Countries. There is a huge disconnection meaning that anything which is unexplainable, indescribable or improbable or not experienced in accordance with the majority is often overlooked as it doesn't relate to the mainstream perspective. It is a very logical approach to only accept things which are scientifically proven. However, there are dimensions beyond logic, and people often experience such dimensions which are very real to them. The intellect or logical approach, which has been the catalyst behind mainstream science for many years has always taken the approach to cut using a sharp knife, for example, a dissection of a flower. It can unquestionably find out a lot of information relating to the flower but cannot really find out the deepest reason as to why the flower is so pretty, or how the flower of life is a great metaphor for evolution in the universe. I am sure we have all experienced love in our lifetime at one stage or another but again, logic cannot describe love. When we look at a glass of water, we know it is H_2O, and we know we drink it to keep hydrated, but do we know what it actually is, and why it is transparent and not another colour instead? We are simply a speck of dust in comparison to the number of galaxies in the Cosmos, so the same can be said about what we know. Dimensions beyond the physical are often timeless so our medical institution, which only has knowledge of the physical body of a human, requires an upgrade so that it is

69

aligned with dimensions of the mind and life energies. Yoga has grasped this truth for thousands of years, and I truly believe it will aid our vitality, especially if encouraged by or aligned with our medical institutions. Until we see this change of approach, people will not be able to advance spiritually as their closest way out of the dark forest is to continue searching for the light at the end of the tunnel, just that extra mile at the end left, but unfortunately many fall short, simply by collapsing near to the finishing line that they don't know is there, or they turn back and go back to life of security or the mundane, which is sometimes behind the prison bars. This will eventually suck the life force out of them, the life force being the positive vibrations of energy. Metaphorically speaking, the dear souls who collapse in the forest are the ones (almost myself had it not been for going beyond that extra mile, with sheer determination, and not listening to external influences) who often listen to their loved ones, relatives and friends who could well be referring to them "as losing their marbles" or "you should see a doctor" or "stop whatever you are doing". The problem with seeing a doctor is that they are only trained on physical aspects and not mental, emotional or spiritual. Anti-depressants which are often subscribed only make the problems more magnified it seems, what with the common, inevitable side effects. Someone who is Schizophrenic, for example, is someone who has mystical experiences, but they are unable to align their mystical experiences with the demands of the world, and they therefore struggle. I was always conscious of this and knew that I had to find a way to align the two in equilibrium. I methodically became curious and passionately obsessed with winning and rising above all personal sorrows, and perspectives of others. This one piece of clarity that I was going to find a way to succeed was all I needed. The intention by which we project out into the universe is boomeranged straight back to us by the correlation of the very nature of its cosmic intelligence. Some refer to it as the "Law of Attraction", and that is exactly what happened as a result. I have since seen life through a whole new lens, and I believe this experience raised my awareness and this is what altered states of consciousness relate to.

We have to follow our knowing within if there is that deep knowing, of course. I suffered significantly when people were concerned for my welfare, as deep down, I knew I wasn't losing it. That deep-down knowing is often referred to as pure consciousness. We all have pure consciousness, when we are consciously witness or observant to our thoughts, emotions, sensations and judgements. What I was experiencing was very real, and when one has no means of connection to someone who can relate to them, then it will require walking on our own through the dark, which we are often conditioned not to do, which is a glitch of our culture in Western Society. We have to face the darkness, in order to transcend the same way a crystal has millions of years of stress in rock form, or a caterpillar's transformation from caterpillar, to cocoon, to butterfly. I believe this is how each find our authenticity, and this is exactly how I view my journey. My authenticity and true self would never have been expressed, nor would I be writing this book had I have listened to the noise all around me, even if it was with empathy or compassion from loved ones. When we have a knowing or a gut feeling, it is often intuitive and powerful guidance. It comes with an element of uncertainty as no one can predict the future, but stepping through amid uncertainty, comes with its rewards. As I have previously mentioned, the Universe reveals its secrets to those in which dare to follow their hearts! I was at the stage where I felt that a loved one, or a relative, or a friend, or a doctor, or a therapist would not be able to help me, as I knew I was having a spiritual experience, something extraordinarily difficult to explain to my family or friends who knew me as the identification that they had come to know all those years. I felt that a doctor only knows the physical dimension, and the Therapist only knows the dimension of the mind, so what was really needed was a spiritual teacher or Healer who knew the concepts of the spiritual or energy dimensions beyond space and time. If we are fortunate enough to find a master or mentor who can calm us, guide us, and help us believe again, then this will do wonders at this particular stage I was in. I did exactly that, I opted to go all the way to Thailand from London to do it! It was early November, the weather was turning wintery, Christmas not yet approached, and my Father said he was going to Thailand for a couple of weeks, so I kind of invited myself, feeling I hadn't got much too lose, although at the time the last person I would ever have thought I would be going on holiday with was my Father! Still to this day, I believe I was guided by the universe. I do not live with my young daughter, the last thing I could think of was to leave her. Anyway, my voice within whispered to go to Thailand. When I first arrived in Thailand, my mind would try to take over from the intuition again. It was a battle between the ego and the spirit. I came to the point of questioning if it was a deceiving demonic entity or some Devi was trying to take over me! What kept me going, was that I began to realise that if I somehow cracked the nut when in Thailand, then maybe, just maybe it would shut up the noise of fear and worry from my loved ones, relatives and friends back home, and I would live another day to tell this story and leave behind some essential footprints to my family, friends and the beloved strangers reading this book, and naturally, my young daughter over whom I was particularly worried and concerned in terms of her future, due to instability in her first years of life thusfar, i.e. her parents separating. If your particular journey resonates with just 10% of what I have just described, then please do everything you can to identify a reputable, or recommended spiritual teacher, master, healer or guru (even if you are an atheist or agnostic like I was). It is either that, or facing the lion's den of judgements, which for sure we all face, and sometimes in a diverse, separated and competitive world we cannot get away from it. That said, no one deserves to be labelled in any way, let alone as "crazy". I could provide you with pages of quotes from Albert Einstein's, and from the greatest sages and prophecies that signal to think outside the box, rather than following the herd, and instead embracing the invaluable time spent in solitude and stillness, often the first steps into ingenious and inventory. This relates to the wonderful journeys of the suffering through to success which the likes of Nelson Mandela and Steve Jobs encountered as a part of their experience. By simply not letting in anyone else's opinions, judgements, beliefs or even their morals (which may not necessarily be moral as such), then you have already won and are acting as the bigger person, although as always, we should view the other/s with loving compassion and forgiveness for your own sake. It is down to one thing and one thing only and that is their own wounds which require healing, so it is essential and recommended we see them through the eyes of love, on a soul level, beneath their personality which they have accumulated as a result of their wounds. On a soul level, everyone is innocent. In your own way, you could prove them wrong, not with a vengeance, but for the sake of moral justice or inspiration. It is amazing how much fuel and emotional juice this creates, but always wish them well and love them as yourself, for separation is an illusion. Even if they are not your brother or sister, they could even be someone you have never met or a troll from social media, but know one thing, they are still at the very deepest level effectively like a brother or sister and is thus an added catalyst for you to now use your "alleged breakdown" as a messaging, inspirational "breakthrough" to that in which chicks naturally break out of their eggshells, such chicks where their ignorance is bliss, not having any awareness, nor any such accumulations of influential external forces preventing the beauty of life. We humans can take a similar approach too.

I believe, gradually, there will come a time when we require the wisdom and support of the spiritual guru less and less, as a good one will have taught an individual that the very basic fundamentals of turning inwards, with patience, is to simply seek and pluck out the answers from within. As we do this, our compulsive desires and cravings begin to dissipate, such as the desire for material possessions of the physical realm, or hoarding onto such item with control, as we will see through a different lens, one in which we notice that both internally and externally we have everything already. It has always been there but many of us have been asleep or in amnesia for too long, and now we are beginning to awaken from the dream. This does take some time to grasp, but why wait when the journey can start today? Most people die without knowing. I have made a personal vow to not be one of them, what you do is entirely up to you. You have been blessed with the power of choice. The power of choice means you can make a difference and do not have to fall victim to circumstance. You can make a heaven out of a hellish situation with the right mindset and rituals which ensure your inner wellbeing. The right choices will manifest into the power of love, it takes years of the wrong choices and continuous, consecutive mistakes and life lessons before our spread of love grows, and of course, the seed of love only starts in one place, like yourself. This is the most beautiful, truest and most sublime aspect of your being.

The higher the consciousness and presence of the individual, the speedier the vibration and the more we realise that time is a construct. We are able to think creatively from a place of love, from an open heart, which emanated from having an open mind. You could use the two as an equation and formula for a beautiful mind. When we have a brilliant mind, it is our soul that is pulling the strings, as we are not cut off from the source. However, when the mind grows weeds, instead of seeds, then this is an indication that the ego has cast its spell over the beliefs and self-worth of the individual, while the intellect sends you down a whole new road altogether! Each of these facets of mind takes the individual beyond the spirit and before you know it, you're in paralysis after a drop of poison entering your cells and manifesting into disease. In this case, the poison is resentment, doubt, fear, worry, and self-pity. This mixture is a tasty mix in the form of alcohol or food as an escape for some people, but of course, it comes at such a price. The human nervous system is compulsive and in disarray. The ego can also deceive us into thinking we are healthy, awake, invincible, awake or enlightened at times, one can seem fine for the moment whilst living in a delusion of being superior, smarter, more morally correct against those around them. One could argue that this is better than pain and suffering associated with the toxicity of the shadow or ego, but really they both exist in partnership, when the intellect gets burned out eventually by going into "fight" or "flight", such as the default status of our 2 million-year-old brain, which is our survival mechanism. After the intellect is burned out, the ego subconsciously takes care of the rest, the individual is now ready to take the next action, by continuing to live in delusion, with that social mask, and when the time is right, the spirit is released. This is an act of grace, which comes forth when we least expect it, this is why it is grace. The best way I can describe grace is that it is something sure which loves us enough to act as our trampoline when we fall down the building! We are able to get back up where we belong. Such an experience makes it impossible to go back to the old you as when you break out of the limiting beliefs and conditioning (which normally indoctrinates fear into the society by large) then you experience pure love and oneness. The surge of energy which rises up the spine toward the crown, through the chakras, is like reaching a train station. This is what is often referred to as reaching gamma brainwaves. When we are in the state of realisation, then time slows down. Linear time is nothing more than a human construct.

The yogis have often remarked that if one touches this state of grace, then the divine becomes the slave to this individual. They are connected to the universe, and the powers of the universe will support this person in reaching their destiny. Synchronicities will appear in the same way a butterfly flickers past you with a blink of an eye. This individual will notice things which others do not. With such a dimension, this person observes how the flower grows, what the role of the ants is, wonders how birds fly, what transfers food such as a banana into a human in a few hours. The person is no different by nature to anyone else, the only difference is that they have dropped all labels and identity to no longer fulfil their society or culture, or the matrix. If our mind and body are solely accumulations of experiences, lessons, memory and the food we eat, then surely there is something pulling the strings in making this process happen.

When an individual begins questioning their society, or become accustomed to seeking and being curious, then they are closer to the source. The same can also be said about the questioning of one's identity in the midst of suffering or trauma or praying for things to improve. Spirit has a way of revealing its love for us, pure divine unconditional love, coming into the limelight when that particular individual in the aftermath of all the seeking, questioning, studying, praying or suffering has finally surrendered to a higher power. Enough is enough for you, and enough is enough for spirit as well, spirit does not at all like the sight of your suffering in the same way a husband doesn't like the sight of his wife in agony during childbirth. This, however, is required as a growth spurt or photosynthetic process just minutes before the holy grail. Imagine, if one day you actually did hear the sacredness of the subtle whispers expressing love, advising you not to give up, informing you that God will always be there when you are close to sinking, and to have faith? Would that not put you at more ease next time you are ready to collapse, not necessarily as the ego will block out your beliefs, faith and hope, it quite literally is back in control if we allow it to, where it feels it has to reside. The ego is narcissistic but when a narcissist is challenged at its root cause, it crumbles and shows up subsequently in service. So no, the act of grace will not make a massive difference other than each time you reach breaking point, you will build up enough of a track record to help you have faith in your next cycle. The toolbox simply contains more tools. By facing each of these tests time and time again, you will have acquired experience, and gathered knowledge, connection, once you have consistently accumulated a few of these cycles. It is then possible for the individual to be passing on these details of such compelling transformation of suffering to fulfilment, fear to courage, onto loved ones or relatives who experience suffering. Often our loved ones or relatives are our most prominent teachers due to their connection with us, even if not always positive. So, we are naturally drawn into wanting to help them first. Think about it, when we receive good news, it is often natural to always want to spread the news with a loved one! This is the healer within us. See, I believe we are all healers but we have forgotten this since ancient times. Although evolution and ascension suggest more people are waking up to realising their innate gifts such as channelling or healing more than ever, the truth is that we are all able to heal ourselves. For example, when after a wound, the body will form a scab over the wound. This is the subconscious intelligence which makes this happen.

In the same way, you can consciously heal as well. Where we went wrong culturally in the modern era is that we allowed the domination of the collective and individual mind to take control and deceive our lives, so many of us haven't been living consciously enough, so our karma although for many of us hasn't been terrible, it hasn't been in best nick either! I am sure you haven't committed murder, it is just that you were a bit all over the place psychologically like I was, like all of us are often times. It is then when the counsellor or therapist is assigned, although with all due respect to them (not that it's their fault, more so the system pulling the strings backstage) they charge a fair amount, but for sure they try their best it's worth noting. It is nice of them to try their best, but their work can be likened to using light staples to pierce through your 100 pages of issues, your wounds from the past that is. A healer, on the other hand, has a larger staple. We have to go well and truly beyond psychology to truly come to terms with peace within. The soul is a whole science in itself. The real goal is for the subconscious mind and conscious mind to be married, so that elevated life force energy takes over from the more hormonal which seeks craving, and into the areas by which interact with laws of the universe.

I take responsibility in the fact that I began this journey being money driven and motivated a tad on titles along the way, I wasn't really keen so much on being famous or a celebrity with millions of pounds to spare as such, I was happy to have enough money to live comfortably with some spare disposable income. I was fortunate enough to have had enough to provide for my young family and we could have one or two pleasant holidays, a nice sports car and lovely apartment in the beautiful, scenic English countryside approximately 1 hour's drive from Central London. As mentioned earlier in the book, this didn't materialise how I had it planned out, or expected. In fact, in life, we always have to change our story or a blueprint of life. Such alteration of our perception is essential otherwise, we will suffer immensely. Life gives us a slap in the face, and it is most definitely a call to change our approach, values or beliefs, or take massive action. I wouldn't want to misguide you and say to you as the reader, that I earn lots now, and live a carefree life every moment of my life, every day. The challenges are always there, but I do have the tools, the tools of fuel, courage, belief and faith to overcome obstacles and challenges almost immediately, striking whilst the iron is hot. The challenges will never go away, but as most of us know, that facing these storms head on really does help us grow in our soul evolution. The eternal spirit can survive any storm in the same way a Himalayan mountain can remain beautiful and stand upright after many earthquakes and landslides!

To fill you in, to one of my current challenges, which requires me to alter and enhance my previous beliefs and general perception, perhaps opening my mind a bit more, is that I notice tonnes of spiritual teachers, healers and gurus charging clients for their time, to heal an individual or a group. It doesn't entirely sit right or add up to me, as on one hand, we all need to make enough money to survive. It goes without saying, but on the other side of the coin, we can view things differently, can't we? For example, many of us in the West are still in the top 20% of the wealthiest people in the world just by living in an MEDC (More Economically Developed Country). The prophets and sages didn't charge to heal, although if they were offered a gift, they would often accept receiving the gift as a non-mandatory donation to allow the individual to experience the honour,

83

privilege and good deed of giving, which will infectiously allow the flow of giving and receiving, often referred to as the Law of Exchange. We have to break out of our selfish ways and realise that the world would go on fine or even better without money, which is a human construct! Unfortunately, the world we live in today, is economically driven, and therefore competition orientated. Many influencers and motivational speakers describe the mechanics of cultivating the Law of Attraction and in receiving financial abundance. This was one of the main teachings I came across upon my early studies. I sit on both sides of the fence, in that yes, of course, we should try to make as much money as we possibly can as we want to be the best we can be in all aspects of life including but not limited to financial abundance, and in the matrix, in the modern-day society, to think of life without there being the exchange of service for money would seem absurd. It has become as normal as fresh air to us, much like pollution has! Financial abundance is not really right or wrong morally, as it is now very normal culturally to naturally seek financial abundance. Speaking of morality, it is how we utilise such spending, and its correct distribution and exchange, which can help people's lives around you for the better, or charitable causes, then it's important to polish up our overall, selfish and compulsive desires and cravings a tad. Once we have a crystal-clear vision, then there is a force beyond our logical thinking part of our mind, which interacts with the intelligence, informational source field of the universe which will bring us away from attachment and obsessive "gold-digging". We will instead attract and receive, not only what we have asked for, but what we deeply deserve and also, yearn for from our soul's desire, in that precise moment. We are all where we are supposed to be at, it cannot be any other way. We are getting what we have asked for, as much as that doesn't seem the case to many of us! We have to alter our perception in order to notice it, that's all. We could be either receiving a lot, or we could be receiving a little. If it is a lot, then spend your birthday money wisely before you lose out on this obligation further down the line, and if it is not much, then you have a deeper purpose and meaning as to why this is happening. Perhaps, you are better than the need for a title, buckets of cash and assets, perhaps you are edging closer to profound insight. The understanding and raised, expanded consciousness that you are already one of the wealthiest humans on the planet, and that it is time to appreciate and be grateful with all your blessings you have previously received. Think about it, so often we fear the worse if we lose our money, but who said you had to have a title in order to be successful? A mother or a housewife has enormous responsibilities and sacred roles, yet they are often just received as "just a mother" or "just a housewife". Who said you have to live in a mansion instead of a beautiful eco-village, who said you have to live in London or New York, whereby you may have a hard time finding an affordable 4-bedroom house, or a flash car to impress your friends? There is nothing at all wrong with luxuries. I appreciate luxuries from to time (Who doesn't? When it is both available and receivable), but only on the basis that it is both balanced and harnessed by also appreciating what the world has already provided us with. We are often too blind to even notice, aren't we? Back to the "who said" rhetorical questions. Who said one would turn homeless in London, from losing it all, as opposed to becoming a monk in the middle of no man's land? You see, we can indeed make the best of absolutely everything. You can bet there is always someone else with a much worse problem. What is a loss of a finger to a person who is quadriplegic, or a child throwing their toys out of the pram with a wild tantrum in front of the parent's neighbours in comparison to a parentless child facing war in Yemen or Syria? Who said one would get more pleasure going to Ibiza, Marbella, Cacoon, or Las Vegas, having an outstanding time, only for a hangover and subsequent, inevitable depression to emerge later, such as the nature of a low straight after a high? Oh, and then checking the bank account the next day, only for it to be running much lower than expected, or empty! This instead, of say, travelling to another country, especially a poorer country where you could learn a new language, a new culture and gain valuable insight into their way of living, and gain perspective along the way. You could even live like a king if you wanted to (with the power of the pound, dollar or euro), or even better you could go and experience a voluntary work exchange or teach English to less fortunate or unprivileged or disabled children. I can guarantee you; you will not need any disposable income for the latter. Don't get me wrong, I still have the same urges to spend on luxury being from the West. Some of us have been bought up close to an Oxford Circus, Mayfair, or Manhattan! People often subscribe to the concept of not forgetting their grassroots, not forgetting who they are, or the origin of their family or birth surname. Yes, in some aspects it is important, as it's great to be proud of your childhood and interests. But again. Let's subscribe to balance and create harmonious effects in our identity. This will only arise when we also dis-identify and dis-label our baggage of past experiences. Just because one is no longer identified as characteristically similar to their family doesn't mean they love them any less or that they are ashamed. Of course, one could still be proud, but the new you, who listens to the heart and its guidance as opposed to external advice and opinions, will cease limiting their self, opening the doorway into limitless potential. Another way of looking at it is that each of us has our own authenticity which is boundless, and therefore our job is to ensure our generation improves the flaws of our ancestors' generation and that we leave our future generations a better place to live in. I believe that the aim of the game is that we are supposed to go beyond our current identity or multiple identities we possess due to accumulation of memory, experiences and the effect of many years of social conditioning. As a child, there is no other way than to be identified with their family, however, as an adult, this individual should grow beyond their biological identity. We all have a biological identity and in essence this is really our most basic identity. Every creature, not just humans, reach a point in which the child turns into a young adult and then the child creates so much tension that one or the other moves out of the house! This is typically the males disagreeing, throwing the weight of their masculinity around (i.e. father and son relationship, but not always). I am not suggesting this is a problem between the parent and child, or more commonly father and son, it is merely two men trying to share the same space. When people live or work with each other, with limited perception, awareness or without understanding one another, then it is common practice for their "fight or flight" mode or survival instinct to be switched on, which causes a fight.

A life of meaning is non-attached to financial abundance, although the door isn't closed to receive. Still, it also has other doors opened in the hallway too, including but not limited to one's health, purpose, relationship, spiritual connection to source, undertaken projects, hobbies etc. The list is endless when one opens themselves up to life. The struggles will always arise but it becomes less severe, and then into a game of chess, where there are some strategic moves required from time to time, along with fairly serious anticipating upon each step especially when there is momentum with attachment to game whilst playing, Monopoly too, that's quite a serious game when one is emotionally invested on each choice they have to make economically, even though it is by a roll of dice. There is no need to take the game so seriously, what a great analogy this is in how we approach life. Mind you, a good game which I never took too seriously is Snakes and Ladders, funny how wherever there is no economics involved, the game becomes less serious, even though snakes and ladders can both become quite dangerous! Sorry I had to chuckle there! Snakes and ladders demonstrate that money isn't the bee all and end all, instead of the analogy it does emphasise is to live on the edge, which is congruent with not taking life too seriously, and instead of viewing life as a game, a play, or even a dance. Sometimes when a child plays, they hurt themselves from having lots of fun every now and then, but they still return to play and get on with their game with exuberance. Maybe we should play Zumba or Charades since life is both a play and a dance!

Being playful is actually being responsible in some respects. It is more irresponsible to walk around in misery and not try to bother one's seriousness and negativity which can be both toxic, and rapidly infectious. This scenario suggests that someone is too attached to their mind and simply needs to detach themselves from their mind. Yoga and Meditation are brilliant for this. The whole of creation and the universe is said to be all energy, it's really a dance of energy all at play. When one tunes into the universe then they naturally are in harmony with the universe, which is all a play, I agree it can also be one big scary rollercoaster at times!

We are either "being" or "doing" in life. The reality is that in today's world, we are doing. Being is what we refer to as vacation, but even today, vacation is still "doing". I can relate to my daughter's first holiday as a baby, bless her! We were put through our paces! In my opinion, based on my experience of doing both, it's essential that we have some time "being" before we are "doing". I think in most cases it is the other way around and often we eventually bite the bullet and opt for that so-called vacation. The trouble is that by the point that time arises, our body has already begun to break down and we are under stress. We need to make "being" a priority. This is when the magic happens. We learn to notice the present more by feeling our senses- being functional, but not restless. Our mind will always play tricks, but less so when we become more still. Beingness slows us down but it is more sustainable in the long run so long as we can beat the addiction which could turn to the road of laziness. That is a joke. I am merely referring to a full-time meditator or monk! By participating in the rat race, one may as well declare they have no faith in the sun rising tomorrow morning! Let's not knock the meditator or monk, for they have not entered the pointless rat-race competition. The truth is that there is both heaven and hell on earth, which do we choose, though? Do we choose to work our guts off continuously for some paper notes and to either spend it on ourselves or our future generations so they can follow in our rat-race footsteps which don't take us too far, only as far as the mouse trap? Or do we instead, execute a life of doing everything we wish to do, where we have had enough time to reflect on our new beliefs, morals, goals, drives, new skills etc. Living a life of "being" doesn't have to be just "being" like the Zen monk. You still have days, weeks, months and even years of "doing", but you are not revolving your whole life to embody the mindset of "I have to live and need enough money to survive". Of course, we need to survive, but one should never forget that 80% of our world lives in poverty. I am currently sitting in a café in India with no Wi-Fi whilst I write this. It is not my place to say who is happy or unhappy out of that 80%, however for anyone who has travelled or stayed in these regions will likely have seen some who are suffering in extortionate pain and desperation and also others who do not have a pot to pee in, that still somehow manage to radiate positivity and a smile in far less than ideal circumstances. Someone else out there is most definitely happy with less than what you or I have, you can bet there are tonnes of people you know that fit into that category too, yet we forget. Why do we forget? Well life is demanding and there is no beating around the bush with that notion.

Perspective serves as a wonderful reminder when we feel we have not reached as per our expectations. Perspective only reminds us when we have stepped away from the 9-5 chaos. If the world is pure energy, then we need to try to use our energy wisely. In the same way, we do not leave the bath tap running with water when we do not need the bath. As a rule of thumb, let's not make our work life more than 30% of our life unless you are one of the fortunate few who truly love their work. Loving your work as if it were your lost love, then maybe committing 100% of your time would be worth its weight in gold! We are all striving for the latter but that will only arise upon time spent in "beingness" as we learn to know ourselves a bit better. We receive clarification in exchange for being more connected within. This is the beautiful and unique functions of the soul, which harbours the present moment. Being is, therefore, what we need, as opposed to doing. That said, there is still such a way, of "being" which flows into every action still.

You are simply a miracle of being. With the right intentions, actions, concentration, you are creating the ultimate balance of the mind, body and spirit. Meditation will further your awakening to liberate the mind, body and spirit complex into enlightenment and cessation of suffering and ignorance.

We should remind ourselves that we are not to blame, neither our parents for any form of ignorance, since we have only been introduced systematically to a 21st century schooling, which emanates from teachings of false religions that do not promote means of "beingness" or spiritual principles which lead to liberation or reunion with the soul. One could argue a strong case that we are effectively like robots plugged into one main machine with controlled capabilities and functions. Otherwise, each robot can become super-capable which endangers the master. The master is a metaphor for the governments.

I have mentioned that we have gifts and talents hidden within, and each of us has a divine purpose behind our existence. So, by spending time in "beingness", we become attracted to these magnets, as such gifts and talents are also seeking us! So, if you now realise you have been overworking and may want to "take life a little less seriously" then you are now closer to knowing something extraordinary. Even if you wish to remain in your dimensionless road, as let's face it, not everyone wishes to pursue an unknown territory, there is no problem with that whatsoever, but please give yourself the most important self-power you could ever give yourself and that is freedom. Freedom has a way of funnelling time and money.

For individuals who wish to head for the pathway to freedom, or the enlightenment, then they take the highway to "beingness" and healing first. The road to enlightenment for those of you who may be aware of being on this path already with great interest may have heard of references to do with the "Third Eye". This terminology refers to the pineal gland for which

I always use the analogy of the appendix where we have been taught by previous old, out of date, mainstream science that it is an irrelevant, minimal functional organism. Today, in modern science, and based on my very own experience and others I have had discussions with, it seems there is a hidden secret about the pineal gland that was a fundamental teaching in many traditions, for example in Ayurvedic philosophy and Yoga, the Ajna Chakra (energy centre above in between the eyebrows) represents the Third Eye. It is also represented in Ancient Egypt as the symbol of the Eye of Horus, which is a spectacularly precise design mirroring the placement of the pineal gland in the profile of the human brain. The pineal gland is pea-size shaped liked a pine cone, located in the vertebrate brain. Mystics consider the Third Eye as the supreme universal connection and the seed of the soul. Modern scientists are now aligning their conclusions with what mystics have claimed for thousands of years. In fact, the significance of the Third Eye seems to appear in every Ancient culture throughout the world. Many statues of prophets and Gods or Goddesses have a third eye. This chakra is believed to be connected to clarity, concentration, intuition and imagination. It is the doorway to all clairvoyance and wisdom. The Egyptians believed one who opened their Third Eye (Eye of Horus) had access to forbidden knowledge, the secrets of the

Gods, and therefore required specialised training by such activation.

There are recommendations and tips for Third eye activation which include but do not limit to the following;

- Avoid consumption of fluoride (often contained bottles of mineral water we drink)
- Meditation and stillness
- Healthy "saatvic" diet, especially Turmeric is known to be useful in particular
- Crystals
- Listening to "Gamma" (hz) frequency music
- Prayer
- Worship

If you are already at this point where you believe you may have already activated your Third eye, then it is essential, if you haven't already, to get in touch with a respectable healer or spiritual teacher or even a Yoga Teacher to give you some more tailored information. If this type of step to discovery and self-realisation is taken without the appropriate and necessary guidance, then there could well be complications. I cannot reiterate the importance of this. If you fill up "diesel" in a petrol car, then there will be consequences.

End of A Beginning

I wrote this book with every ounce of blood, sweat and tears pouring down as glowing, pure white bright light, a ray of loving energy to spring every cell of my dear daughter into life, in her growth throughout her lifetime. In the same way, similarly, that very spark of grace one day touched my old self and erased the darkness and lack of life within my cells, to an upgrade to all my restrictive biology that had been holding me back from adventure. I feel my cells have sprung to a degree of aliveness and purpose to work together with other cells in the same way we grow in our aliveness and purpose, in nurturing and constructing solid relationships to create in union with others, stepping away from lack, terror, resentment, sabotage, judgement and fear. We are merely cells to our universe. So, this scenario I have explained refers to the day I woke up from the dream, discovering that I am more than my body. I am a multi-dimensional mind, body, spirit complex having this human experience. Even if I am wrong, there is more wellness, conscious eating, better relationships and less fear on my part, so that is something that suggests the growth and ascension activation when the illusion becomes a realisation of one's awareness. Nothing is ever that easy anymore, as before. However, it's certainly not as harsh or nor is there an injustice as a victim playing out in blame and finger-pointing, opening new cans of worms, instead there is more acceptance for the overall experience of this thing we call life. Moving on from the lows, as if they are now "high-lows". I offer my prayer and faith to every single soul who reads this book or comes into contact with you as a family member or relative as well. Please know that this was in no way to preach. I was raised in South London, whereby I always wondered why there was so much pressure to earn, to acquire a mortgage and going back to early childhood I do remember racism at school, and so much hatred towards certain religions and cultures, not to mention the bullying as well. All of this because of division and separation. Quite possibly because of the belief systems many of us ascertained from our parents and the peer pressure of friends at school. School, for me, was war. War is purely separation, and there was a fight for peace amongst our teachers, but peace is not something we can combat. The more we fight it, the more it manifests. The only way it stops is purely the inner journey, going within that is. The rest will gradually improve, the external will mirror the internal, it always does. The war I faced at school always stayed with me in the memory of my subconscious and has had a bed-bug effect on my DNA and although I had forgotten about it when I left school, and like many teenagers and young adults, had begun to party, and get up to all sorts of mischief.

What came to follow was adulthood and responsibility, barely having any disposable income and subsequently struggling to keep my head above water when it came to having to pay my bills and the pressure of providing for my young family. This all felt so too familiar, so similar to the order and robust nature of school. Judgements, left, right and centre. Groups and classes divided via I.Q. and regrettably certain minority groups in the lesser I.Q. groups, which could be linked to their religion, skin colour, ability to speak the English language or wealth of one's family home. Every pupil would often compare their grades and capabilities socially, or which football team to support, or who made the football or cricket team? Whoever didn't simply wasn't worthy of interacting with that particular group of individuals. The teachers knew this but there wasn't much they could do. They just advised not to bully or physically, or psychologically harm each other, they would offer the odd incentive in exchange for disciplined behaviour but it wasn't enough. We had 300 pupils in our grade, things used to get really out of hand in the school playground! I am sure the teachers used their best endeavours; however, they were only as good as the curriculum itself. As I said, we can fight against war by fighting for peace all we like but it won't change anything. Ultimately the way the mind works is that what you resist persists. Imagine the collective mind worldwide when every group views their own morals and views to be the right approach. School kids and generations of adulthood are no different in that respect. Meditation and stillness on the hand is a call to change something inwards and to translate those insecurities into strengths and new meanings, living with passion resulted. The outside factors and circumstances will not change unless we heal and care for ourselves within. We have to self-love in order for things to really blossom. This was a major school teaching in ancient times, and most definitely, there is a requirement for this to happen in our current era now. I believe we are already ascending in our evolution which is very much reliant on embodying love. To embody love and share this gift with others, this powerful, high vibrational emotion; we first have to understand the mechanics of stripping away fear and conditioning, and then self-love will come into fruition. Yoga in some ways is similar to meditation There are various Asanas and Postures, although the breathing techniques relate. The origin and age of both practices also relate. Yogis are often informing us that Yoga is purely about union and looking beyond the illusion that we are all separate from one another, not just with humanity, but for all such life forms within the cosmos. For example, we are inhaling what the trees exhale, and the trees are inhaling what we exhale. Likewise, the food we consume and eat effectively becomes a part of us. How can there genuinely be separation when there is clearly, sharing, inter-connectivity amongst all of nature, a process in which everything affects one another. Yet we are living in times when we compete with each other, backstab each other at school, at the workplace, in fact, where I am from, literally stab each other. This is society today, and it is in our best interests to realise we are all the same since we breathe the same air and oxygen, bleed the same colour red, and feel the heavy burden of pain or suffering from time to time. I will end this book by saying that we all carry this invisible Goddess embryo inside each of us, much like awakening the genie within. We have been conditioned to think this is just some fantasy. There is a part of us which is buried deep within, something timeless. It resides in our heart but is luminous. In Yoga this is often referred to as Kundalini, simply evoking that sleeping giant within. Kundalini is linked with our right-sided brain, where the pineal gland resides. It is no different to having an underlining software program in our minds that tells us what we have to get to the next level of our lives. I needn't reveal any more as you have already started your journey by successfully reaching the end of this book. The seeds of wisdom and love are already hidden as a treasure in your being, buried deep beneath your physical body. Nobody is neither inferior nor superior, just the expression of pure consciousness and the divine. You get to choose your very own Heaven or Hell by understanding your inner engineering and human mechanics. You are only able to perceive what you have mapped in your brain what you have experienced neurologically and emotionally. Altering your perception filters your beliefs, which alters your attitudes, which then alters your feeling and thoughts, and lastly your memory and experiences. It is all linked like a chain. You are both mortal and immortal simultaneously. Mortal on the physical plane, but immortal on the astral plane. Marcus Aurelious has a famous quote which I try to affirm daily; "What we do now echoes in eternity". All this wisdom you have gathered and accumulated ensures that you have no obligation to your former self. Pave the way for the new, authentic, one and only you with no such false limiting beliefs or labels, and merely your limitless potential to love, grow, achieve, share. The going will get tough and you will continue to be tested to your limits no matter where you are on your journey, so re-affirm the notion of the warrior within slaying its demons, that's right, my friend. You and I are both our own worst enemy like every single human on the face of this earth, so face this inner mess with pure surrender and faith that the situation will improve and the storm will pass. Change yourself today from low vibrations of survival to high vibrations of creation, where you are able to cultivate your body and mind in its proper means, as an instrument. The essence of existence is not about money and title, rather it is about becoming a steady source of wellbeing within by realising the innate gifts and implementing conscious choices to bring you all the freedom. This is what heaven really is, in Earthly terms, not something outside of ourselves. We can beat pain, strife and adversity in every sense of the word, regardless of circumstances, by merely cultivating pure loving thoughts instead of pathological thinking, that is a nice easy trade-off when we come to think of it. Why are we so worried about money, or someone else's competition or jealousy in our lives, we will all die one day, and as such, our clothes, and jewellery will exceed their shelf life! I believe our collective mission is to learn and to love even under the most traumatic of situations, so that if we are going through hell, we will be able to see the golden thread that weaves through the situation or experience, triggering and restoring that gateway to heaven which is nothing more than pure love. We have come here to live and there is no other purpose and this is most fundamental. Thinking that there is a better place than this Earth is a crime. It is because of this we have destroyed so many things here. If we do not figure out that we are here to learn and love, then we fall into the trap of the Law of Karma. Most of us fall into the Law of Karma without realising. It is really no different from unconscious behavioural patterns. We are not doing anything bad deliberately or necessarily out of spite, it is just that we have taken ownership of our level of consciousness and executing conscious action. Conscious action normally doesn't result in neglect in behaviours of love, compassion and service. We are here to learn from our mistakes, attain meaning, not for money or fame. We have an obligation to our soul and to others, for there is no such thing as true separation, only unified consciousness. We are all of the same energy. You are a tiny droplet of water in the ocean. It's all the same, depending on how you perceive it, and how you perceive has everything to do with your level of consciousness. Your divine essence has become enslaved, just like mine and everybody's. This sacred energy is guiding you every step of the way, the moment you become aware of this is the moment it starts to show up to your school play, it will parent you if you let it! Such awareness of this beautiful notion enables you to make choices which free you, realising which one can become a producer, rather than a consumer of life. No more bending backwards to a society that doesn't serve your best interests at heart, but instead helping society with its glitches.

The world really is your oyster now as you have enhanced level of knowledge and profound awareness, although that is up to you whether you have chosen to accept the events and experiences of this story, it is your own free will, so you can choose whether to throw this information away as garbage, or feed your mind with it. If you choose the latter, then I invite you to join me by investing in ourselves and the end goal in changing the paradigm for future generations so that they don't have to face the same roadblocks to our success and wellbeing as we have encountered. It is your closest ally in a world living in an illusion of separation.

If someone could tell us, right at the start of our lives that we are dying, then we might live life to the limit, every minute of every day. Tomorrow is an illusion that hasn't yet occurred nor is it a foregone conclusion, so go do the things you love and that which your soul harbours, so long as they do not cause harm for those around you. Irrespective of circumstances, I think the Creator gave you a fair deal there. Everyone has a piece in life's puzzle. Withdraw into the cocoon of extraordinary self-love and before you know it, you will be the butterfly that lightens up someone's day and makes hearts melt, being the vessel of love that you are. Whatever you do, whether you believe it or not, I would like you to know one thing, that you will always be loved wherever you go, since we are all a work in progress. You are safe to be wild. You have got this, my dear brother or sister!

May love, light and blessings come your way and stay pertained. May peace prevail.

Thank you, thank you, thank you!

Sam

Made in the USA
Monee, IL
01 March 2022

92093047R00069